Language Development Activity Book
with Standardized Test Practice

4

ScottForesman

Accelerating English Language Learning

Authors

Anna Uhl Chamot

Jim Cummins

Carolyn Kessler

J. Michael O'Malley

Lily Wong Fillmore

Consultant

George González

ScottForesman

Editorial Offices: Glenview, Illinois
Regional Offices: Sunnyvale, California • Atlanta, Georgia
Glenview, Illinois • Oakland, New Jersey • Dallas, Texas

ISBN 0-673-19696-8
ISBN 0-673-19704-2 [Texas]

1900 East Lake Avenue, Glenview, Illinois 60025.
  5 6 7 8 9 10 CR 05 04 03 02 01 00 99 98 97

Contents

What a Job!

Draw a line to match each picture with a job.

 1.    a. teacher

 2.    b. rancher

 3.    c. pilot

 4.    d. policewoman

 5.    e. miner

 6.    f. fisherman

 7.    g. farmer

8.    h. nurse

What's in the picture?

A. Look at the picture. Complete each sentence with the correct number word and the correct singular or plural word. See the example.

Example: There is _____one_____ _____house_____ in the picture.
                              house/houses

1. There are _____ _____ in the picture.
                              rancher/ranchers

2. There is _____ _____.
                              child/children

3. There are _____ _____.
                              horse/horses

4. There are _____ _____.
                              tree/trees

5. There is _____ _____.
                              mountain/mountains

B. Write a sentence. How many cows are in the picture?

_____

What do they do?

A. Choose a verb for each sentence.

1. Many people _____ a living by farming.

        earn / eat

2. Some farmers in California _____ strawberries.

        grow / earn

3. Some people in Wyoming _____ on ranches.

        work / wear

4. Some ranchers _____ a lot of cattle.

        live / raise

5. Some people in the West _____ cowboy hats and boots.

        wear / grow

6. Many people_____ grapefruits from Texas.

        eat / earn

B. Draw a picture for one of the sentences.

Name _____

Which one doesn't belong?

Place an *X* on the word that doesn't belong in each group.

Fish

tuna   salmon
bicycle   mackerel

Metals

copper   book
iron   silver

Things Made of Silver

spoon   fork
cup   pencil

Things Made from Petroleum

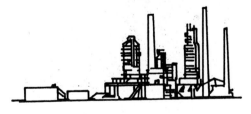

gasoline   oil
pot   fuel

Western States

New York   California
Texas   Oregon

5

The *m* and *n* Sounds

A. Underline the words in each paragraph with an *m* sound. Circle the words with an *n* sound. Some words will be both underlined and circled.

Some people live near the ocean. People who fish catch millions of pounds of fish.

They catch tuna and mackerel. They also catch salmon.

Other people in the West are miners. They mine copper, iron, and silver. Copper is

used in pennies. Silver is used in spoons. They also mine petroleum. Petroleum is

used in gasoline.

B. Work with a partner. Practice saying the words you circled and underlined.
   Then take turns reading the paragraphs.

Name _____

Singular or Plural?

A. Write the correct word on the line.

1. The truck _____ the gasoline to the gas station.
   take / takes

2. People _____ their cars to the gas station.
   drive / drives

3. They _____ gasoline in their cars.
   put / puts

4. Gasoline _____ their cars go.
   make / makes

5. Some people _____ trips in their cars.
   take / takes

6. Jamie _____ her car to a farm.
   drive / drives

7. She _____ potatoes from the farmer.
   buy / buys

B. Write a sentence. Tell where someone drives a car.

_____

Cactus Clothes

Look at the items on this page. Fill out the order form.
Show and tell a partner what you ordered.

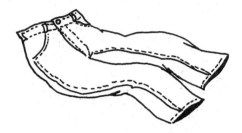

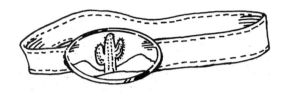

Order a pair of our comfortable
Western jeans today!
Price: $29.95 each
Colors: blue, black, white
Sizes: 10, 12, 14

Your jeans will look great with
one of our Western belts!
Price: $10.95 each
Colors: blue, black, white
Sizes: small, medium, large

Name _____

Address _____

City _____ State _____ Zip Code _____

Phone Number _____

Clothing Item	Color	Size	How Many	Item Price	Total Price

Name _____

Solve it!

Choose words from the box to finish the puzzle.

cattle	farms	mountains
cowboys	mines	ranches

1. Many mines are dug here.
2. These people wear Western boots and belts.
3. Ranchers raise these animals.
4. People raise cattle here.
5. People grow crops here.
6. People dig for silver and copper here.

Math Objectives: Demonstrate an understanding of probability and statistics.
Use the operations of addition, subtraction, multiplication, and division.

Clues

1. Some questions may ask you to look at information in graphs to determine possible outcomes or explain the information. Do not choose answers that are not reasonable.

2. When you try to solve problems using addition, subtraction, multiplication, or division, you should make a quick estimation by rounding off the number.

Sample

The graph shows the favorite horses of students at Sam Houston Elementary School.

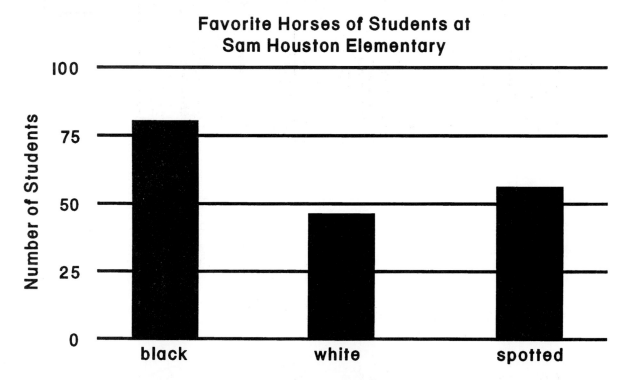

Favorite Horses of Students at Sam Houston Elementary

About how many students chose the black horse as their favorite?

Ⓐ 125

Ⓑ 75

Ⓒ 100

Ⓓ 90

Your best choice is **B.** The graph shows a little more than 75 but is not near enough to 100 to be 90.

Name _____

Try It!

Directions

Read the question carefully to figure out what information you need to find.

Favorite Western Shop Purchases

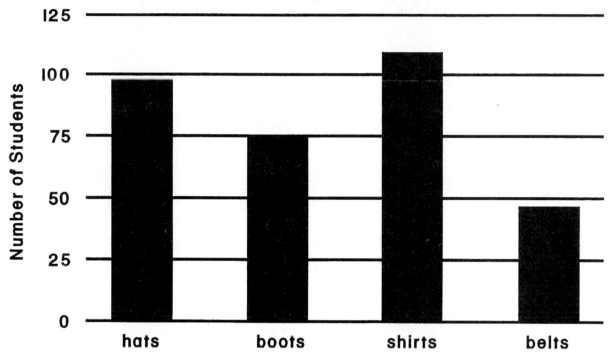

1. Which two items did most of the students like the best?
   - (A) shirts and belts
   - (B) hats and shirts
   - (C) hats and belts
   - (D) boots and hats

2. 462 − 342 =
   - (A) 120
   - (B) 220
   - (C) 140
   - (D) 240

3. If shirts cost $29 each, how much would 2 shirts cost?
   - (A) $50
   - (B) $49
   - (C) $40
   - (D) $58

4. 63 ÷ 9 =
   - (A) 6
   - (B) 9
   - (C) 7
   - (D) 8

What do they want to do?

A. Use the pictures to tell what each person wants to do.
Choose an answer from the box.

to eat a sandwich	to read a book
to go to the movies	to ride a bicycle
to play soccer	

1. Jane wants _____.

2. They want _____.

3. Betty wants _____.

4. Toshi wants _____.

5. Dan wants _____.

B. Write a sentence to tell what you want to do.

_____

Things from Home

The words in the box name things the settlers packed in their covered wagons.
Use a word fo finish each sentence.

books	chairs	pots	soap
candles	hammers	scissors	toys

1. The settlers took furniture such as tables and _____ .

2. They took cooking supplies such as _____ and pans.

3. They took _____ to help them see at night.

4. They took _____ so they could wash.

5. They took needles, thread, and _____ to make clothes.

6. They took _____ and nails to fix things.

7. The children took their favorite _____ to play with.

8. People took their favorite _____ to read.

The *w* Sound

A. Circle the words with the *w* sound. Say the words you circled.

1. very   wagons   water

2. west   used   will

3. want   wet   visit

4. under   would   write

5. wake up   were   valley

B. Complete each sentence with a word you circled.

1. The settlers traveled in covered _____ .

2. They took some food and _____ .

3. People traveled _____ for many reasons.

C. Write a sentence with one of the words you circled.

_____

_____

What *would* Ana do?

A. Write sentences to tell what Ana *would* do last year. See the example.

Ana usually got up at 7:00 A.M

Ana would get up at 7:00 A.M. _____ .

1. She usually ate breakfast at 7:15.

_____ .

2. Then she usually walked to school.

_____ .

3. In school, she usually studied English every day.

_____ .

4. Ana usually arrived home from school at 3:30 P.M.

_____ .

B. Now write two sentences like the ones above to tell what you usually did last year. Use *would* in the second sentence.

_____

_____

What did they say?

A. Look at what each person said. Then complete each sentence.
Remember to add quotation marks and a period.
See the example.

Juanita said, _____ "I'm happy today." _____

1. Ron said, _____

2. Mrs. Gold said, _____

3. Mr. Valdez said, _____

B. Answer the question below. Remember to use quotation marks.

What would you say if you won a million dollars?

I would say, _____ .

In the Past

Use the verb from the first sentence to complete the second sentence.
Add -ed to show that something happened in the past.

1. We **want** to play soccer today.

   We _____ to play soccer yesterday too.

2. We always **cook** our own food.

   Last night, we _____ meat and potatoes.

3. The boys always **bake** their bread on Saturday.

   Yesterday, they _____ three loaves.

4. They usually **clean** the house in the morning.

   Last week, they _____ in the afternoon.

5. Sometimes, the boys **fish** in the river.

   Yesterday, they _____ in the lake.

What a Feeling!

A. Put an exclamation mark (!) at the end of each word or sentence that tells a strong feeling. Put a period (.) at the end of each sentence that does not tell a strong feeling. See the example.

I am nine years old ___.___

1. Come quickly _____

2. I live on the prairie _____

3. The prairie is flat _____

4. What a surprise _____

5. Fire _____

6. We are in school _____

7. Wow _____

8. They cooked their own food _____

9. Help _____

B. Write one sentence of your own to tell a strong feeling. Remember to put an exclamation mark at the end.

_____

Unscramble it!

A. Unscramble the words. Write one letter in each space.

1.

tainsmoun

2.

orhses

3.

erriv

1. __ __ ☐ __ __ __ __ __ __ __

2. __ __ ☐ __ __ __

3. __ __ __ ☐ __ __ __

4. __ __ ☐ __ __ __

5. __ __ ☐ __ __ __

6. __ __ __ ☐ __ __ __ __

4.

wonag

5.

ctoas

6.

banektsl

B. The letters in the boxes spell a secret word. Write the secret word in the sentence.

The settlers traveled west on the _____ Trail.

Social Studies Objective: Demonstrate an understanding of geographical concepts and information.

Clue

Some questions will ask about landforms, climate, and how people of the past adapted to their physical environment. Other questions will ask about geographical locations.

Sample

Many of the early settlers moved west

(A) to find a big city

(B) to see mountains

(C) to find gold or silver

(D) to see wild horses

If you think about what many people who went west did, you will know that **to find gold or silver** is the correct response.

Name _____

Try It!

Directions

Read each question and all of the possible responses carefully. Mark the response that best answers the question.

1. Where did most of the settlers who moved west start their journeys from?

   (A) England, Ireland, and Japan

   (B) the eastern states, Germany, Russia, Norway, and Sweden

   (C) the eastern states, Italy, Brazil, and Egypt

   (D) the northern states, Spain, Portugal, and Africa

2. How long did it often take the settlers to travel west in their covered wagons?

   (A) three to four weeks

   (B) two years

   (C) ten days

   (D) six to eight months

3. How did people traveling west prepare for their long trip?

   (A) They packed only food and water.

   (B) They packed everything they had.

   (C) They packed the things they would need: clothes, furniture, food and water, soap, and so on.

   (D) They packed only toys, books, and family pictures.

4. Where were fires a common problem for the settlers?

   (A) on the prairies

   (B) in the mountains

   (C) near the lakes

   (D) in the East

How does it sound?

A. Read each word.

Write /k/ if the letter *c* in the word has the /k/ sound, like in *cat*.

Write /s/ if the letter *c* has the /s/ sound, like in *cent*.

Then take turns saying each word with a partner.

cell _____   car _____

city _____   certain _____

could _____   microscope _____

active _____   pencil _____

center _____   dance _____

B. Use one of the words above to complete each sentence.

1. All living things are made up of _____.

2. A _____ makes things look bigger.

3. I need a _____ to write.

4. Los Angeles is a large _____ in California.

5. When I hear music, I want to _____.

Name _____

Living or Nonliving?

A. Read the words in the box.

Find and circle each word across and down in the puzzle.

bird	book	boy	flower	fungus	house	iron	lizard	rock	silver

```
h  b  f  u  n  g  u  s
s  i  l  v  e  r  h  d
i  r  o  n  o  m  r  j
h  d  w  a  k  o  b  b
o  e  e  m  t  n  o  o
u  t  r  l  m  n  y  o
s  h  m  a  r  o  c  k
e  l  i  z  a  r  d  p
```

B. Write each word from the box in the correct column.

Living Things	Nonliving Things

Right Now!

A. Complete the second sentence in each pair.

Use *am*, *is*, or *are* and the *-ing* form of the verb in the first sentence.

See the example.

In the summer, the sun shines almost every day.

The sun _____is shining_____ right now.

1. Most plants make their own food.

   This plant _____ food right now.

2. Plants use the sun's energy to make food.

   These trees _____ the sun's energy right now.

3. Many animals eat only plants.

   The rhinoceros _____ a plant right now.

4. People use yeast to make dough for bread and buns.

   I _____ yeast right now to make bread.

B. Complete this sentence to tell what you are doing right now.

   I _____ right now.

Name _____

What and *How*

A. Use the words in the box or your own words to answer the questions.

a bicycle   by bus   happy   play soccer
put meat on bread   two o'clock

1. How do you get to school? _____

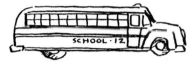

2. What time is it? _____

3. What do you do after school? _____

4. How do you feel today? _____

5. How do you make a sandwich? _____

6. What do you want for your birthday? _____

B. Write two questions for a partner to answer.

1. What _____ ?

_____ .

2. How _____ ?

_____ .

Sound it out!

A. Work with a partner to say each sound out loud.
   Then draw a line to match each sound with the thing that makes it.

1. meow

2. hiss

3. quack quack

4. roar

5. beep beep

6. tick tock

7. buzz

8. splash

a.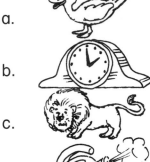

b.

c.

d.

e.

f.

g.

h.

B. Write one more word to name a sound.
   Draw a picture of the thing that makes the sound.

Things They Do

A. Look at the pictures.

Use the words in the box to tell what Sam does with his family.

cooks dinner	*listens to music*	*plays cards*
plays football		*reads a book*

1. Sam _____ with his brother.

2. Sam _____ with his father.

3. Sam _____ with his sister.

4. Sam _____ with his mother.

5. Sam _____ with his grandfather.

B. Write one thing you do with someone in your family.

_____

What Animals Do

A. Tell what the animals cannot do. Tell what the animals do. Use the picture clues.
   Choose your answers from the box. See the example.

builds a nest	dance	eats	plays
read	rests in winter	sings	write

A bear cannot _____ write _____.

It _____ rests in winter _____.

1. A bird cannot _____.

   It _____ and _____.

2. A cat cannot _____.

   It _____ and _____.

B. Write about your favorite animal.

   Tell what it cannot do and what it does.

A _____ cannot _____.

It _____.

Crossword Fun

Use the clues and the words in the box to solve the puzzle.

| air | cells | energy | fungus | language |
| living | | microscope | splits | yeast |

Across

2. A _____ is a plant that doesn't make its own food.

5. People use _____ to communicate.

8. You need a _____ to see cells.

Down

1. Birds, grass, and babies are all _____ things.

3. When a cell gets bigger, it _____.

4. All living things need _____ to grow.

6. Plants use water, sun, and _____ to make food.

7. People use _____ to make dough for bread.

9. All living things are made of tiny parts called _____.

Science Objectives:
1. Demonstrate the ability to acquire scientific data.
2. Demonstrate the ability to make inferences and form generalized statements or predictions using scientific data.

Clues

1. Some questions will ask you to make inferences or generalizations from data or information given.

2. Other questions will ask you to identify appropriate equipment or material or measure length, weight, or changes over time.

Sample

Which picture shows a seed in its last stage of growth?

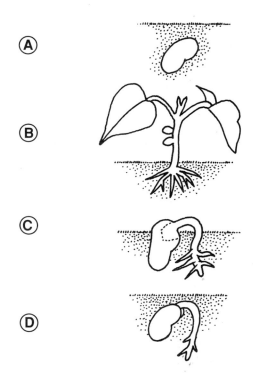

Ⓐ

Ⓑ

Ⓒ

Ⓓ

B is correct! Over time, the seed becomes a full-grown plant.

Name _____

Try It!

1. About how long is this fish?

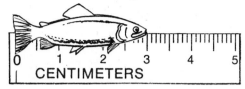

   Ⓐ 4.0 centimeters

   Ⓑ 3.5 centimeters

   Ⓒ 4.5 centimeters

   Ⓓ 3.0 centimeters

2. Over time, what will this become?

   Ⓐ a frog

   Ⓑ a fish

   Ⓒ a turtle

   Ⓓ an earthworm

3. Which answer shows the change in the tree from autumn to spring?

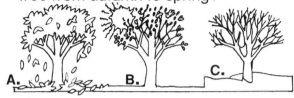

   Ⓐ B, A, C

   Ⓑ C, B, A

   Ⓒ A, C, B

   Ⓓ C, A, B

4. Predators are animals that hunt other animals for food. Which of these is a predator?

   Ⓐ butterfly

   Ⓑ squirrel

   Ⓒ bird

   Ⓓ tiger

Comparisons

Read each pair of sentences.
Use a word from the box to complete the second sentence.

deer	feather	mouse	rock	snow

1. Tina will carry the box by herself.
   It's as light as a _____ .

2. I can't eat this candy.
   It's as hard as a _____ .

3. Elena will win the race.
   She runs as fast as a _____ .

4. Alicia doesn't talk very much.
   She's as quiet as a _____ .

5. Look at the beautiful cloud.
   It's as white as _____ .

When and As

A. Use *when* to make two short sentences into one long sentence.
See the example.

I go to the beach. It is hot.
I go to the beach when it is hot.

1. She eats an apple. She is hungry.

_____

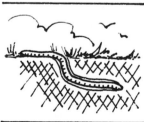

2. I carry an umbrella. It is raining.

_____

B. Use *as* to make two short sentences into one long sentence.
See the example.

The earthworm makes a tunnel. It crawls through the soil.
The earthworm makes a tunnel as it crawls through the soil.

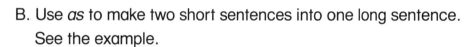

1. My feet leave footprints. I walk in the sand.

_____

2. Maya takes notes. She listens to the tape.

_____

Words with /oi/

A. Read the words in the box with a partner.

Write the missing letters that spell /oi/ in each word.

| boy | coin | enjoy | moist | noise | poison | soil | toy |

p _____ _____ son   c _____ _____ n

t _____ _____   b _____ _____

n _____ _____ se   enj _____ _____

s _____ _____ l   m _____ _____ st

B. Use a word from the box to complete each sentence.

1. Sara is playing with her new _____.

2. Did you hear that loud _____?

3. The _____ in the blue shirt is Rajib.

4. Earthworms live in the _____.

5. The ground is a little wet. It feels _____.

6. Don't drink that. It might be _____.

7. I always _____ going to parties.

8. A nickel is a _____.

How many? How much?

A. Look at the pictures. Complete each question with *How much* or *How many.*
Write a sentence to answer each question.

1. _____ puppies are there?

_____

2. _____ cells do you see?

_____

3. _____ does it cost?

_____

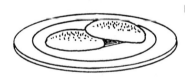

4. _____ cookies does he always eat?

_____

5. _____ glasses of water should you drink
each day?

_____

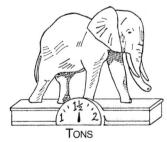

Tons

6. _____ does it weigh?

_____

B. Write a question with *How much* or *How many.*
Ask a partner to answer your question.

_____

_____

Where is it?

Look at the picture.
Use words from the box to finish each sentence.

beyond	in the center of	into	near	on

1. The island is _____ the lake.

2. The mountain is _____ the island.

3. The boat is sailing _____ the lake.

4. The deer is running _____ the forest.

5. The tree is _____ the island.

6. The boat is _____ the island.

Combine Sentences

Read the pairs of short sentences.
Use *who* to make one long sentence from the two short sentences.

See the example.

The old ladies liked cats. They helped the cats.

_____ The old ladies who liked cats helped the cats. _____

1. The sailors sailed around the island. They kept the island safe.

   _____

2. The sailors drank a lot of milk. They were strong.

   _____

3. The invaders came one night. They destroyed the town.

   _____

4. The people had cats. They didn't have mice.

   _____

5. The cows had little clover to eat. They gave poor milk.

   _____

What They Must Do

A. Read each sentence. Write what the people must do.
   Choose an answer from the box.

clean it up	help her	look both ways
practice	study hard	

1. Mary, your room is a mess!

   You must _____ now.

2. Tomorrow Heath will have a big test in school.

   He must _____ tonight.

3. Gloria's mother has a lot of work to do.

   Gloria must _____ this afternoon.

4. Amir wants to be a good soccer player.

   He must _____ every day.

5. Brown Street is a very busy street.

   You must _____ before you cross.

B. Write two things you must do today.

I must _____.

I must _____.

What am I?

A. Unscramble these words. Write them on the line.

1. rthworema   _____

2. neltun   _____

3. eocsymest   _____ _____

4. oils   _____

5. lammma   _____

B. Use the words you unscrambled to answer the three riddles.
   Draw a picture for each answer.

I live in dirt.

I eat soil and dead plants.

What am I?

_____

I have hair and a backbone.

I am warm-blooded.

What am I?

_____

I am dirt.

Earthworms dig tunnels in me.

What am I?

_____

Name _____

Science Objective: Demonstrate the ability to draw conclusions about the process or outcomes of a scientific investigation.

Clues

1. Some questions will ask you to predict the outcomes of actions based on experiences or data.

2. Other questions will ask you to draw conclusions from observed data.

Sample

If an apple tree is planted in soil, what else will it need to grow?

Ⓐ sun and dirt

Ⓑ sun and worms

Ⓒ soil and water

Ⓓ sun and rain

Did you choose **D**? You are right. All plants need to have sun and water to grow. The rain provides the water.

Try It!

Directions

Read each question carefully. Mark the best answer.

1. If Marco wants to see how many earthworms live in 2 gallons of soil, what is the first thing he should do?

   Ⓐ Dig up some dirt and look for worms.

   Ⓑ Count worms as they crawl out of the soil.

   Ⓒ Get a 2 gallon container and fill it with dirt from the yard.

   Ⓓ Sit and wait for the worms to come out.

2. Marisol wants to see fungi grow. What is a good source for this experiment?

   Ⓐ flowers

   Ⓑ old bread

   Ⓒ potato chips

   Ⓓ grass

3. What part do mosquitoes and grasshoppers play in the bat's ecosystem?

   Ⓐ They are friends of bats.

   Ⓑ They give bats oxygen.

   Ⓒ They look for food for bats.

   Ⓓ They are a source of food.

4. What would happen if you put a healthy plant in a closet for two weeks with no light and you watered it every day?

   Ⓐ It would probably grow.

   Ⓑ Its leaves would fall off.

   Ⓒ Its roots would grow longer.

   Ⓓ It would probably die.

Resources

A. Look at the Indian shelters. Write the name of one resource that was used to build each shelter. Use the words in the box.

bark	clay	skins	snow

1. This shelter is made of _____.

2. This shelter is made of _____.

3. This shelter is made of _____.

4. This shelter is made of _____.

B. Draw a picture of a home where you live.
   Name one resource that was used to build it.

This shelter is made of _____.

Who are *they?*

Read the sentences. Circle the people or things the word *they* refers to.
Example: (Students) are in class. They are reading.

1. Long ago, many Indians lived in North America.

   They were the first Americans.

2. American Indians found many resources.

   They built shelters from the resources.

3. Look at the pictures.

   They show American Indian shelters.

4. The Inuit lived in cold areas.

   They built houses of snow.

5. The Aztecs lived in Mexico.

   They built adobe houses.

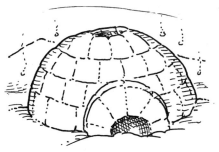

6. Read the pages.

   They tell about the American Indians.

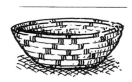

What is it used for?

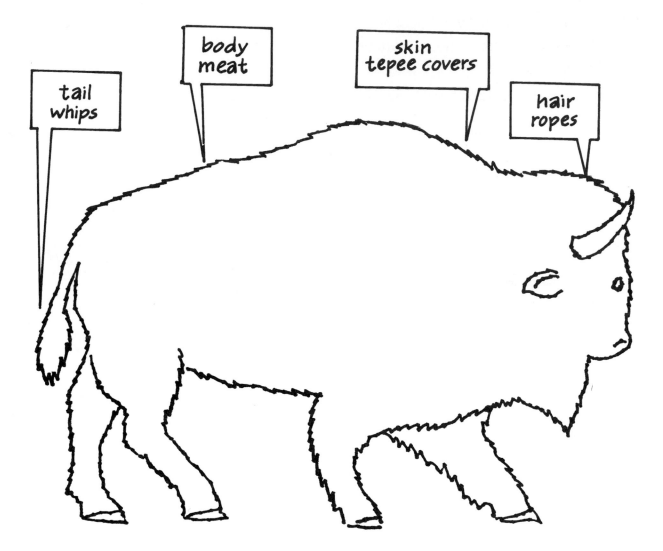

tail whips

body meat

skin tepee covers

hair ropes

A. Look at the picture of the buffalo. Complete the sentences. Follow the pattern.

   1. The Plains Indians used the buffalo tail for _____.

   2. The Plains Indians _____ buffalo hair for _____.

   3. The Plains Indians used the body of the buffalo _____ _____.

   4. The Plains Indians _____ buffalo skin for _____.

B. Write a sentence. Tell what the Indians used the buffalo for.

_____

_____

What have they done?

Read what archaeologists have done.
Write *have* and choose a form of the verb in ( ) from the box.
See the example.

| dug | found | learned | seen | studied |

Archaeologists ___have___ ___learned___ how American Indians lived long ago.
(learn)

1. They _____ _____ some ancient pottery.
(see)

2. Archaeologists _____ _____ up many things
from the ground. (dig)

3. They _____ _____ American Indian tools.
(find)

4. Archaeologists _____ _____ the things they
found. (study)

Name _____

How was it used?

Look at each picture. Read the word.
Write the word in the correct column in the chart.

Pottery	Tools	Weapons

pot

scraper

hammer

arrowhead

cup

knife

First or last?

A. Look at the picture. Read the question. Write the name.

1. Who is first? _____

2. Who is next? _____

3. Who is third? _____

4. Who is last? _____

B. Write about one child in the picture.

What is the child doing? Where is the child?

_____

_____

_____

_____

_____

You must be . . .

Complete the sentences. Write *must be* and a word from the box on each line.

happy	hungry	sad	sick	tired

1. Kim: I didn't eat much for lunch.

   Lin: You _____.

2. Tim: I got a good grade on the test.

   Dad: You _____.

3. Ron: I didn't get much sleep last night.

   Paul: You _____.

4. Anita: I feel warm and my ear hurts.

   Mother: You _____.

5. Deb: We lost the soccer game.

   Sue: You _____.

Name _____

How does it sound?

A. Read the sentences. Circle the twelve words that begin with the /j/ sound.

1. Pam is wearing a yellow jacket and jeans.

2. I enjoy jumping rope and jogging.

3. Alan took the jar of cherry jam.

4. Janet and I rode in a jeep in Yosemite Park.

5. You can join our group in the gym.

6. Have you seen a giraffe on a jet yet?

B. List all the /j/ words you circled.

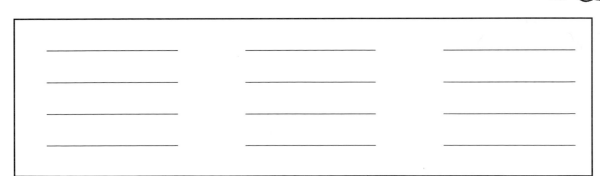

_____   _____   _____

_____   _____   _____

_____   _____   _____

_____   _____   _____

C. Work with a partner. Take turns reading each sentence.

Reading Objectives: Identify cause and effect.
Make inferences.

Clues:
1. Words such as **because, since,** and **made** indicate cause.
2. Think about what the question is asking you to find. You can answer cause-and-effect questions by thinking about how one thing can make something else happen. You can make inferences by looking for clues in pictures or in sentences.

Sample:

Think about rain. What are some of the things that can happen if it rains?

•You will get wet if you go outside.

•Traffic accidents might happen because of wet roads.

•Plants will grow.

What happens if there is too much rain?

•There might be floods.

•The soccer field will be too wet for people to play soccer.

1. Rain is good because
   - Ⓐ you can get wet.
   - Ⓑ it makes plants grow.
   - Ⓒ floods can happen.
   - Ⓓ it makes soccer fields wet.

2. When a soccer field is too wet,
   - Ⓐ the field may be too dangerous to play on.
   - Ⓑ grass grows too quickly.
   - Ⓒ people can't play because they will get wet.
   - Ⓓ players can't score goals.

1. **It makes plants grow** is your best choice. All of the other answers may be information in the passage. But make sure you are choosing the answer that the question asks.

2. **The field may be too dangerous to play on** is the best choice. We can infer from the statement that people don't play soccer on wet fields because they may have accidents.

Name _____

Try It!

Directions:

First, quickly read the questions to see what information you will be looking for as you read. Read the passage. Answer each question by finding the best answer.

The Big Quarrel

Many years ago, the Birds and the Animals had a big quarrel. The Birds thought that those who had wings were better. The Animals thought that those with teeth were better. They argued so much that it looked like they would have a war soon. Crane and Bear had an idea to play a ball game instead. The loser would have to accept a penalty that the winner chose.

Bat was a creature who was very confused. He had both teeth and wings. Which group would he choose for his team? Since Bat was so little, the Birds laughed at Bat when he flew to their side. The Animals didn't want Bat either because he had wings. Finally, Bear let Bat join the Animals in the game.

At the game, Crane and Hawk often stole the ball when the Animals got close to the goal. As it got dark, it was harder for both the Birds and the Animals to score because they couldn't see. But Bat could see at night, so he stole the ball from Crane. Then Bat flew between the poles to score.

Because Bat helped the Animals win, they let him set the penalty for the Birds. Their penalty was to leave that land for half of each year. So when you see a flock of birds flying together, you will know that they are serving their penalty.

1. The Animals and Birds were about to have a war because
   Ⓐ each group thought they were better.
   Ⓑ both wanted the land.
   Ⓒ each had their own parts.
   Ⓓ their feelings were hurt.

2. Bat was not accepted on the Animals' or the Birds' teams because
   Ⓐ he was never at the practices.
   Ⓑ he was always a bad sport.
   Ⓒ he was a little different from both of them.
   Ⓓ the coach didn't like him.

3. After the game, the Birds
   Ⓐ had to leave the forest.
   Ⓑ had to serve a penalty.
   Ⓒ couldn't play ball.
   Ⓓ had to accept Bat.

4. Bat was able to score because
   Ⓐ he had teeth.
   Ⓑ he was faster than the birds.
   Ⓒ he was little.
   Ⓓ he could see at night.

In the Past

A. Complete each sentence. Write the past tense of the verb in ( ).

1. The Aztec farmers _____ many crops.
   (grow)

2. Some Aztec farms _____ in the highlands.
   (are)

3. Cotton and papayas _____ from farms in the lowlands.
   (come)

4. Farmers from the highlands _____ their crops to market.
   (take)

5. They _____ their crops for things they needed.
   (trade)

B. Write a sentence about the Aztecs. Use a verb in the past tense.

_____

Name _____

What will you trade?

Work with a partner. One of you is a highlands farmer. One of you is a lowlands farmer. Cut out the pictures of your crops. Trade your crops.

Say: I'll trade you some of my _____ for some of your _____ .

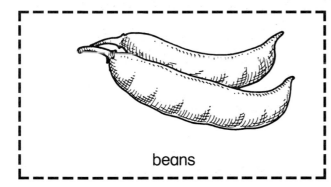

beans

potatoes

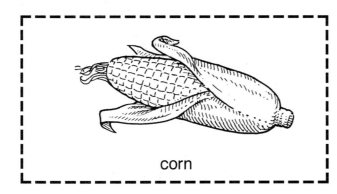

corn

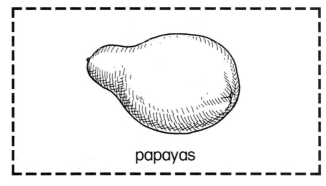

papayas

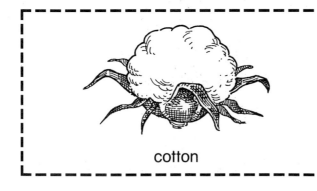

cotton

cacao beans

Words with /st/

A. Circle the word with /st/.

1. This flower has a   stem / shrub / leaf.

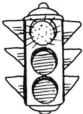

2. A red light means   go / stop / slow.

3. This is a pile of   rocks / stones / sand.

4. This is my favorite   book / song / story.

5. Look at the   sky / stars / clouds.

B. Work with a partner. Take turns reading the sentences to each other. Make sure to use the words you circled. Then practice saying all the words you circled.

Name _____

What do you like?

Ask your friends these questions. Write their names in the chart.

1. Do you like chocolate?

2. Do you like tomatoes?

3. Do you like tacos?

4. Do you like chili peppers?

Food	Who likes it?	Who does not like it?
chocolate		
tomatoes		
tacos		
chili peppers		

Solve the problem.

A. Use the calendar to answer the questions.

| February |
Sun	Mon	Tue	Wed	Thurs	Fri	Sat
						1
2	3	4	5	6	7	8
9	10	11	12	13	14	15
16	17	18	19	20	21	22
23	24	25	26	27	28	29

There are many holidays in February.

President Abraham Lincoln's birthday is two days before Valentine's Day.

Valentine's Day is on February 14.

When is President Lincoln's birthday? _____

President George Washington's birthday is eight days after Valentine's Day.

It is ten days after President Lincoln's birthday.

When is President Washington's birthday? _____

On this calendar, Ramadan begins one week before President's Day.

Ramadan begins on February 10.

When is President's Day? _____

B. Use the calendar to make up your own math problem.
   Trade papers with a partner. Solve the problems.

_____

_____

Before or After?

Complete the sentences. Write *before* or *after*.

1. Cinco de Mayo is four days _____ May Day.

2. Tina's birthday is one week _____ Victor's birthday.

3. Mother's Day is _____ the class trip.

4. The class trip is four days _____ the school play.

5. The class party is one week _____ the play.

6. Two days _____ the school picnic is Mother's Day.

When did it happen?

Complete the sentences. Write *when* or *then*.

1. _____ Coyote got hungry, he would eat his turkeys.

2. Coyote ate all of the turkeys, and _____ he ate the sheep.

3. _____ the sheep were all gone, Coyote started to eat the horses.

4. _____ there were no horses left to pull his plow.

5. _____ the dogs saw what was happening, they had a meeting.

6. They decided to go, and _____ they all ran away.

Math Objectives

1. Demonstrate an understanding of number concepts.
2. Demonstrate an understanding of mathematical relations.
3. Demonstrate an understanding of geometric properties and relationships.
4. Demonstrate an understanding of geometric properties.

Clues

1. We can use squares to show groups of numbers. Each ☐ stands for 1. This is called base ten.
2. Some of these questions will ask you to identify and describe shapes, find missing elements in patterns, or identify congruence and symmetry.
3. Other questions will ask you about time, length, weight, and temperature. You will need to know how the clock works and how you use a ruler and scales. You will need to know that a thermometer measures temperature.

Sample

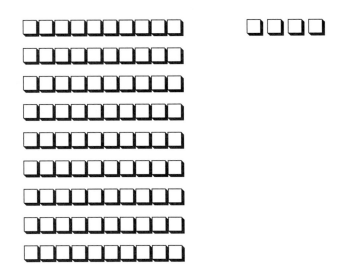

Look at the base ten blocks. If 3 tens are taken away from the tens group, what number will be shown?

  (A) 24
  (B) 64
  (C) 74
  (D) 21

The correct answer is 64. Three tens equal 30 to be subtracted from 94.

Name _____

Try It!

1. What is the missing number in the number pattern?

   4, 11, 18, 25, _____, 39

   Ⓐ 32

   Ⓑ 28

   Ⓒ 33

   Ⓓ 38

2. Find the perimeter of this square. (The *perimeter* is the distance around something.) Clue: All four sides are the same length.

    3 meters

   Ⓐ 6 meters

   Ⓑ 12 meters

   Ⓒ 13 meters

   Ⓓ 9 meters

3. Carlos played soccer for 1 hour on Monday, Wednesday, and Friday. How many minutes did he play?

   Ⓐ 100 minutes

   Ⓑ 120 minutes

   Ⓒ 80 minutes

   Ⓓ 180 minutes

4. Which number sentence is in the same family of facts as 4 x 7 = 28?

   Ⓐ 4 + 7 = 11

   Ⓑ 28 ÷ 7 = 4

   Ⓒ 14 + 14 = 28

   Ⓓ 28 - 7 = 21

Name _____

I can!

Complete each sentence about you.
Draw a picture to go with each sentence.

1. When I was five, I could _____.

2. When I was five, I couldn't _____.

3. Now, I can _____.

4. When I am twenty, I will be able to _____.

1.

2.

3.

4.

What do they need?

A. Choose a word from the box to finish each sentence.
Use each word only once.

bed	book	food	water

1. Ana is sleepy.

   She needs a _____ to sleep.

2. They are thirsty.

   They need _____ to drink.

3. We are hungry.

   We need _____ to eat.

4. Daniel wants to study English.

   He needs a _____ to read.

B. Write two sentences about things you need.

I need _____ .

I need _____ .

What did they do?

A. Look at the pictures. Write a short answer for each question.
   See the example.

Did Steven eat an apple?

_____ No, he didn't. _____

1. Did they ride their bikes?

   _____

2. Did Pedro walk to school yesterday?

   _____

3. Did Lily read a book?

   _____

4. Did Luis play soccer today?

   _____

B. Write two questions using *did*.
   Ask a classmate to answer your questions.

_____ ?

_____ ?

Name _____

Choose a balanced diet.

A. Work with a partner.

Write down lunch and dinner foods for a balanced diet.

Lunch   **Dinner**

B. Put each food in the correct food group on the Food Pyramid.

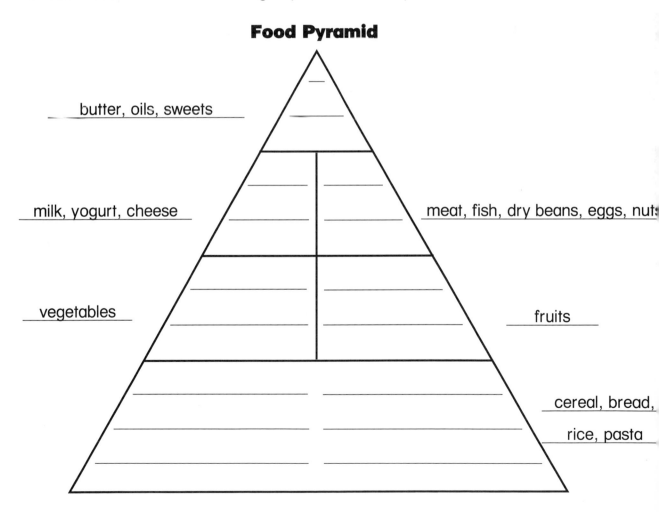

Food Pyramid

butter, oils, sweets

milk, yogurt, cheese   meat, fish, dry beans, eggs, nut

vegetables   fruits

cereal, bread,

rice, pasta

C. Did you choose more foods from the bottom of the Food Pyramid? _____

What food is it?

Match the name of the food with the picture.

1. orange

2. apple

3. rice

4. corn

5. banana

6. carrot

7. egg roll

8. ice cream

9. pizza

10. pear

a.

b.

c.

d.

e.

f.

g.

h.

i.

j.

Well or *Poorly*

A. Write the word *well* or *poorly* to complete each sentence.

1. Oranges grow _____ in Florida.

2. Jamie writes _____.

3. Susana sings _____.

4. Pedro plays the trumpet _____.

5. Dan plays soccer _____.

B. Write about yourself.
   Write a sentence to tell one thing you do well.

_____.

What's the sound?

Each word in the box has the /yü/ sound in *beautiful* or the /ü/ sound in *soup*.
Listen as your teacher reads each word. Decide which sound it has.
Write the word in the correct column.

boot	food	mule	tool	use
cute	moon	ruler	united	usually

/yü/ in beautiful   **/ü/ in soup**

1. _____   1. _____

2. _____   2. _____

3. _____   3. _____

4. _____   4. _____

5. _____   5. _____

Name _____

All About Food

Find and circle the following words across and down in the puzzle.

balanced diet	fats	nutrients
carbohydrates	food pyramid	proteins
energy	minerals	vitamins

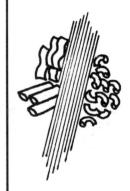

```
B A L A N C E D D I E T
A C I J F A T S S D A N
D D E N E R G Y T N T S
E G H M I B D V E U U R
B P J I O O M I V T V O
P R Q E K H L T E R R N
F O O D P Y R A M I D W
C T X B G D A M O E D H
E E Y R A R Z I N N A A
D I E G M A W N X T Y R
F N I H T T U S V S Z R
E S M I N E R A L S P Y
L K J S R S C A R O L Q
```

Name _____

Reading Objective: Determine meanings of words.

Clues
Sometimes you can find the meaning of a word in the text.
Word meanings may be in the same sentence as the word.
Word meanings also may be in the sentence before or
after the word.

Sample
Many kinds of food smell divine. The pleasant smells make you
want to eat more and more. Fruits and vegetables always smell
fresh. They have a lot of vitamins in them to help you grow strong.

1. In this passage, the word
   divine means

   ○ spicy

   ○ juicy

   ○ pleasant

   ○ smelly

2. Which would you choose to
   get vitamins to help you
   grow?

   ○ soda and a candy bar

   ○ ice cream cone

   ○ pizza and soda

   ○ vegetables and fruits

Food could be spicy, juicy, or smelly, but
the passage describes **divine** as a
pleasant smell.

All of them sound great, but **vegetables
and fruits** is the best choice to have a
healthy body that grows.

Name _____

Directions:
Quickly look at the questions before you read. Read the passage.
Then mark the best answer choice.

Food for You

Your body needs some food every day. The food you eat gives your body energy. Energy helps you walk, run, play, eat, and talk. Your bones and muscles grow stronger when you eat foods with nutrients. You need these ingredients every day.

You might like only a few kinds of food, but you need nutrients from many kinds of foods. You need a balanced diet of proteins, carbohydrates, and fats. A food pyramid is a chart that shows which foods are better for you than others. The bottom of the pyramid lists the foods that are the best for you. The top of the pyramid lists foods that you don't need as much of.

1. **Energy** is
   Ⓐ many kinds of food
   Ⓑ walking, running, playing, and talking
   Ⓒ strength for walking and other activities
   Ⓓ eating three times a day

2. The **ingredients** in food that help you are
   Ⓐ nutrients
   Ⓑ bones and muscles
   Ⓒ vegetables
   Ⓓ eating and talking

3. The **food pyramid** is
   Ⓐ a chart of foods
   Ⓑ an energy triangle
   Ⓒ a balanced diet
   Ⓓ proteins and fats

4. Which of these foods can you add to make this a balanced meal?
   Ⓐ a soda
   Ⓑ a piece of cake
   Ⓒ carrots
   Ⓓ potato chips

Digestion

Use the words in the box to label the diagram.
Write the correct word on the line.

esophagus   saliva   stomach
large intestine   small intestine

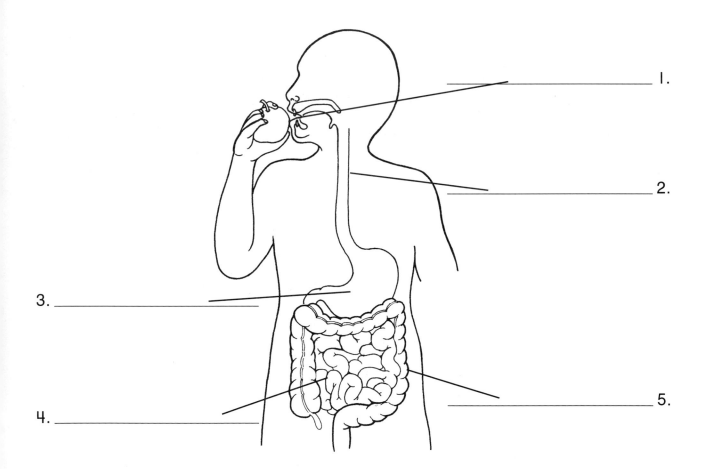

I. _____

2. _____

3. _____

4. _____

5. _____

When does it happen?

A. Draw a line to match the activity and when it happens.

1. Debra goes to bed

a. when he is happy.

2. Ron eats fruit

b. when she is thirsty.

3. Betty drinks water

c. when I want to play.

4. Manuel smiles

d. when she is sleepy.

5. I go to the park

e. when he is hungry.

B. Name an activity you do and tell when you do it.
Draw a picture for your sentence.

I _____ when _____.

Twist and Bend

A. Read about your stomach.

After you eat, your stomach is full.
Your stomach muscles twist and bend.
They mix and digest the food.

Two hours after you eat, your stomach still has some food in it.
Your stomach muscles keep twisting and bending.

Four hours after you eat, your stomach is empty.
But your stomach muscles keep twisting and bending.
They make a rumbling sound telling you it's time to eat again.

B. Work with a partner to answer the questions.
   See the example.

Do your stomach muscles twist and bend after you eat?
Yes, they do. _____

1. Does your stomach still have food in it two hours after you eat?

   _____

2. Does your stomach still have food in it four hours after you eat?

   _____

C. Write a question with *do* or *does* for your partner to answer.

   _____

   _____

What's the secret word?

A. Write the word for each picture.

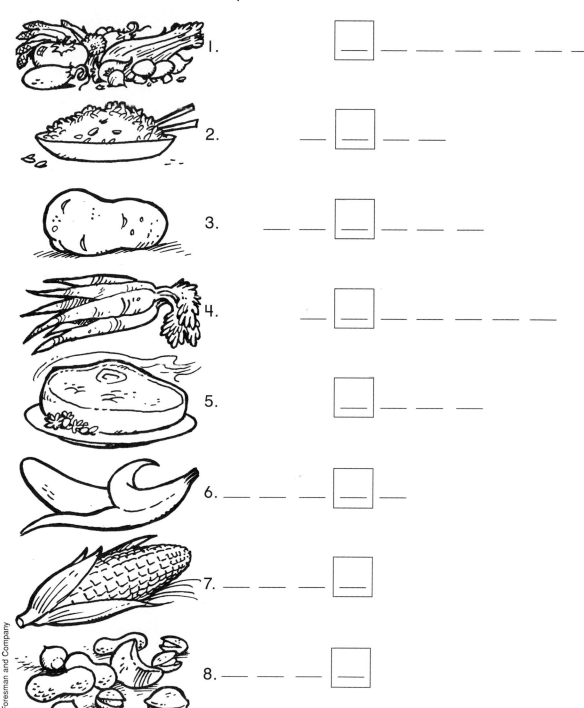

1. [ ] – – – – – – –

2. – [ ] – –

3. – – [ ] – –

4. – [ ] – – – – –

5. [ ] – – –

6. – – – [ ] –

7. – – [ ] –

8. – – – [ ]

B. Look at the letters in the boxes. What word do they spell?

– – – – – – – –

Vanna and Boris

A. Read the conversation.
   Circle the words with the sound of *v* like in (very.)
   Underline the words with the sound of *b* like in *boy*.

1. Vanna: Are you hungry, Boris?

   Boris: Yes, I am hungry.

2. Vanna: Have some bananas and some vegetables.

   Boris: Thank you, Vanna.

3. Vanna: Carrots are good for you. They have Vitamin A.

   Boris: Oh, really?

4. Vanna: Do you like strawberries?

   Boris: Yes, I do.

5. Vanna: Strawberries have Vitamin C.

   Boris: Can I have some strawberries?

   Vanna: Sorry, Ben just ate them.

B. Read the conversation with a partner.
   One of you can be Vanna, and the other one can be Boris.

I should.

Read the story.

> My name is Inés.
> I should do three things at home.
> First, I should do all my homework.
> Second, I should listen to my parents.
> Third, I should help my younger brothers and sisters.

B. Write about yourself.

What three things should you do at school?

Draw a picture of each thing you should do.

> First, I should _____ .
>
> Second, I should _____ .
>
> Third, I should _____ .

Where are they?

Look at the picture.

Imagine you are standing on a balcony of an apartment building.

Write words from the box to complete the sentences.

Use each answer only once.

across   down below   in the distance   next to   on

1. The park is _____ the street.

2. The woman is _____ the balcony.

3. The mountains are _____ .

4. The bank is _____ the park.

5. The children are _____ the balcony.

What do they like?

A. Choose a word from the box to complete each sentence.

| chicken | hamburgers | ice cream |

1. María and Carlos like _____.

2. Sam likes _____.

3. They all like _____.

B. Choose a word from the box to complete each sentence.

| dance | eat | sing |

1. Ana likes to _____.

2. Sarah and José like to _____.

3. They all like to _____.

C. Tell about yourself.
   1. What food do you like?

_____.

   2. What do you like to do?

_____.

Writing Objectives

1. Respond appropriately in a written composition to the purpose/audience specified for a given topic.

2. Organize ideas in a written composition on a given topic.

3. Demonstrate control of the English language in a written composition on a given topic.

4. Generate a written composition that develops, supports, and elaborates the central idea stated in a given topic.

Clues

On the actual test, you will be asked to write only one of these kinds of compositions:

A. Write a composition to describe an object, a person, a place, a situation, or a picture.

   Example: Write a composition to describe your classroom.

B. Write a composition to tell how to do something.

   Example: Write directions to tell your friend how to make a sandwich. Make sure you include all the steps.

C. Write a composition to classify ideas, objects, or people.

   Example: Write what is good and what is bad about having to ride the bus to school.

D. Write a composition to convince an audience of your point of view on a particular issue.

   Example: Your principal is thinking about removing the soda machine from the cafeteria. What is your point of view? Convince your principal to see your point of view.

Try It!

Directions

Choose one of the four kinds of compositions from the Clues section on page 80. Write your composition on the lines below.

Here are some hints about how your writing will be scored on the test.

1. You will not be penalized for grammar mistakes unless there are so many errors that the reader cannot understand what is written.

2. Your score will not be affected by spelling errors unless there are so many errors in familiar words that the reader cannot understand what is written.

3. Your score will not be affected by punctuation errors.

4. Scoring will be lowered for the following:

   a. a written response that doesn't follow the type of composition chosen

   b. a written response that is too short

   c. a written response that does not stay on the topic

   d. a written response that has gaps, or is missing something

   e. a written response that does not communicate clearly

_____

_____

_____

_____

_____

_____

_____

_____

_____

_____

_____

Where are they?

Look at the picture.
Write a word from the box to complete each sentence.
Use each word only once.

above	along	below	through

1. The jaguar is sleeping _____ the tree branches.

2. The parrot is flying _____ the tree.

3. Manuel is running _____ the river.

4. Pak is walking _____ the door.

Can you give examples?

Look at the picture.
Choose two words from the word box to complete each sentence.

apples	bananas	baseball	beetles
butterflies	monkeys	snakes	soccer

1. There are many animals in the rain forest, such as

   _____ and _____ .

2. My friend and I play many games, such as

   _____ and _____ .

3. There are many insects in the rain forest, such as

   _____ and _____ .

4. Every day I eat a lot of fruit, such as

   _____ and _____ .

Name _____

Nouns and Pronouns

Read each pair of sentences.
Circle the words that the underlined word replaces.

1. Rain forests are hot.
   <u>They</u> grow in warm and sunny places.

2. The sun shines twelve hours a day.
   <u>It</u> gives plants energy to help them make food.

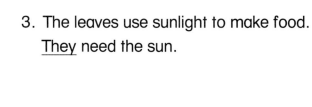

3. The leaves use sunlight to make food.
   <u>They</u> need the sun.

4. Solar energy moves from species to species.
   <u>It</u> moves from the plants to the animals.

What's the sound?

Circle the words that begin with the *l* sound.

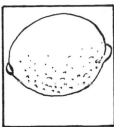
lemon

tree

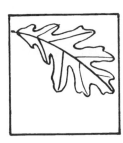
leaf

spider

Circle the words that begin with the *r* sound.

rock

rice

apple

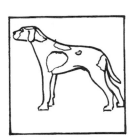
dog

Make a list of words you know that have the *l* sound.

_____   _____

_____   _____

Make another list of words you know that have the *r* sound.

_____   _____

_____   _____

Compare your lists with a friend's lists.
Take turns reading your lists to each other.

Comparisons

Draw a **big** animal, a **bigger** animal, and a **biggest** animal and label them.

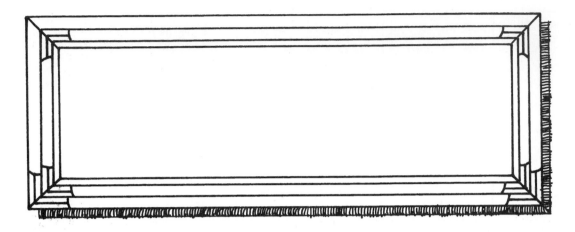

Draw a **long** snake, a **longer** snake, and a **longest** snake and label them.

Draw a **short** person, a **shorter** person, and a **shortest** person and label them.

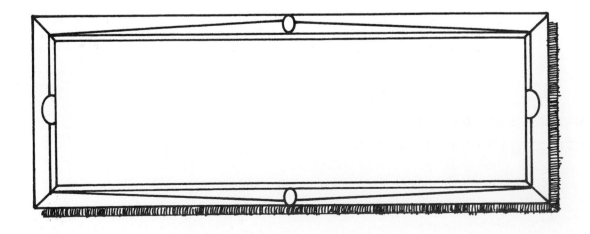

How often does this happen?

Tell about what happens in a tropical rain forest.
Put a check in the correct box.

	Always	Usually	Sometimes	Never
It rains.				
The sun shines.				
It snows.				
People collect latex.				
Plants grow.				

Now tell about yourself. Finish each sentence.

1. I always _____.

2. I usually _____.

3. I sometimes _____.

4. I never _____.

Present or Past?

Read each sentence. Choose the best answer.
See the example.

 It ____rained____ yesterday.

rain/rained

 1. Today, I _____ in the United States.

lived/live

 2. I _____ to the park yesterday.

go/went

 3. I _____ English every day now.

studied/study

 4. Last night, we _____ dinner at seven o'clock.

eat/ate

5. _____ you like to play football after school now?

Do/Did

What's the solution?

A. Use a word from the box to complete each sentence.

Africa	equator	temperature	tropics	twelve

1. A rain forest needs a _____ _____ each day of about 81 degrees.

2. A rain forest needs _____ hours of sunlight each day.

3. Most rain forests grow in the _____ .

4. The _____ is an imaginary line around the middle of the earth.

5. There are rain forests in Central America, South America, Asia, and _____ .

B. Use each answer word in the puzzle.

© Scott, Foresman and Company

Reading Objectives:
1. Summarize a variety of texts.
2. Recognize points of view or statements that are fact or non-fact.

Clues
1. Some questions will ask you to find the main idea, which is the most important idea of the passage. Other questions will ask you to give a summary, which is the main idea with some important details included.

2. Some questions will ask you to think as the author thinks about something. Other questions will ask you to decide between fact or non-fact. Remember, a fact is something you can prove by looking back at the passage.

Sample

Many plants and animals live in the world's rain forests. Some of them can't live in any other environment. One of the most important jobs of the rain forest is to produce oxygen for all of us to breathe. People are destroying many rain forests by cutting or burning. In 100 years, scientists think that the rain forests will be gone.

An important job of the rain forest is

     Ⓐ to grow plants.

     Ⓑ to protect animals.

     Ⓒ to produce oxygen.

     Ⓓ to produce rain.

Did you find your answer in the passage? It's **C.** It is stated in the third sentence.

Name _____

Try It!

Directions

Read the questions before you read the passage. After reading the passage, mark the best answer choice for each question.

The Forest Trail

If you took a trip along a rain forest trail, you would see many birds, animals, and plants. You might see three types of monkeys—the howler, the woolly, and the capuchin.

If you were in a rain forest, you might hear birds communicating in different ways. The pica pau, or woodpecker, calls out from a tree to let the animals in the forest know when someone is present. Uru birds sing when summer has arrived. The tinamou sings a song at the same time every day. That is the mother tinamou's signal to begin the evening meal before it gets dark.

For many years, people who have lived in rain forests in South America have used some of the rain forest plants for medicines. Avocado pits make a tea that is good for swelling if you step on a tucandera ant.

1. The best summary for this passage is

Ⓐ There are many birds, plants, and animals in the rain forest. Different types of birds have different ways of communicating. Many plants are good for medicine.

Ⓑ The rain forest has ants and stingrays that will sting you. You can use an avocado pit to help the swelling.

Ⓒ South Americans have been using medicines from the rain forest for many years.

Ⓓ There are four kinds of monkeys in the rain forest.

2. Which of these is not a fact in the passage?

Ⓐ Avocado pits can help swelling.

Ⓑ South Americans have used plants for medicine.

Ⓒ Tucandera ants sting.

Ⓓ The rain forest is a beautiful place.

Name _____

Why are trees important?

Match the wood product with its name.

1. pencil

2. ruler

3. desk

4. paper

5. house

A.

B.

C.

D.

E.

Draw some other wood products and label them. Show them to a friend.

Name _____

/tr/ and /gr/

A. Choose a word from the box to name each picture. Write it on the line.
   Circle the pictures of the words with /tr/.

apple	leaf	parrot
ten	tree	truck

1. 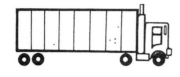   

_____ _____ _____

2.      

_____ _____ _____

B. Circle the pictures of the words with /gr/.

glove	grapes	grass
lizard	pencil	ruler

1.       

_____ _____ _____

2.

_____ _____ _____

In the Past

Complete each sentence with the past tense of the verb in (   ).
See the example.

The trees _____grew_____ very tall last year.
                (grow)

1. I _____ to school yesterday.
        (run)

2. Ana _____ her book under the desk.
          (find)

3. The farmer _____ a lot of corn last year.
             (sell)

4. They _____ the new road two months ago.
          (build)

5. Paul _____ the answer on his paper.
         (write)

6. People _____ that the rain forest had many trees.
          (think)

7. Yesterday, my dad _____ down a tree.
           (cut)

Rain Forest Things

The words in the box name things that come from the rain forest.

avocado	bananas	cashews	chocolate	cinnamon
coconuts	oil	pineapples	rubber	vanilla

Find each word in the puzzle and circle it.

b	c	i	n	n	a	m	o	n	p
r	h	b	p	v	x	s	i	b	i
t	o	v	a	n	i	l	l	a	n
z	c	d	f	g	r	o	n	n	e
c	o	c	o	n	u	t	s	a	a
a	l	r	u	b	b	e	r	n	p
s	a	v	o	c	a	d	o	a	p
h	t	s	x	w	m	n	t	s	l
e	e	a	a	g	s	u	h	i	e
w	y	l	h	u	v	t	z	r	s
s	f	k	h	p	e	s	d	k	c

What do you think it is?

Look at the picture. What do you think it is?
Write a sentence telling what you think it *might* be.
Use the word *might* in your sentence.

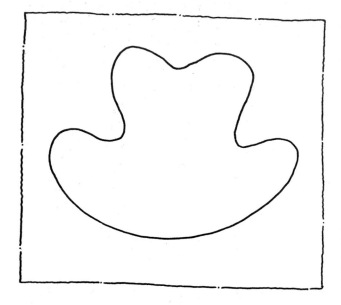

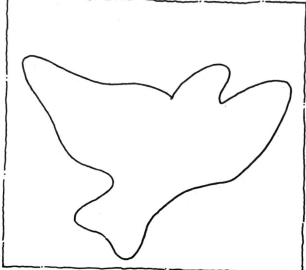

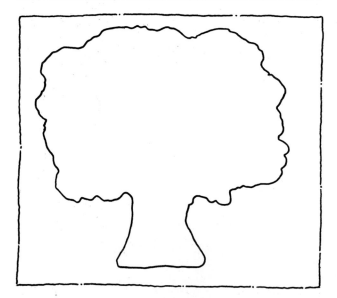

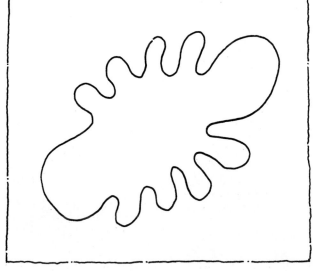

What is happening?

Look at the picture.
Use *is* or *are* and the *-ing* form of the verb in (   ) to answer the question.
See the example.

What is the bug doing?

The bug _____**is eating**_____ the leaf.
(eat)

1. What is the woman doing?

She _____ the tree in the rain forest.
(study)

2. What are these monkeys doing?

They _____ on a tree.
(swing)

3. What is the carpenter doing?

He _____ a table.
(build)

4. What is the parrot doing?

It _____.
(talk)

Write a cinquain poem.

A cinquain poem has five lines and eleven words.
Use the instructions below to help you write one.

Line 1: Write the word *Trees* as your title.

Line 2: Write two words to describe trees.

Line 3: Write three words to tell how trees help you.

Line 4: Write four words to tell how you feel about trees.

Line 5: Write the word *Trees* again.

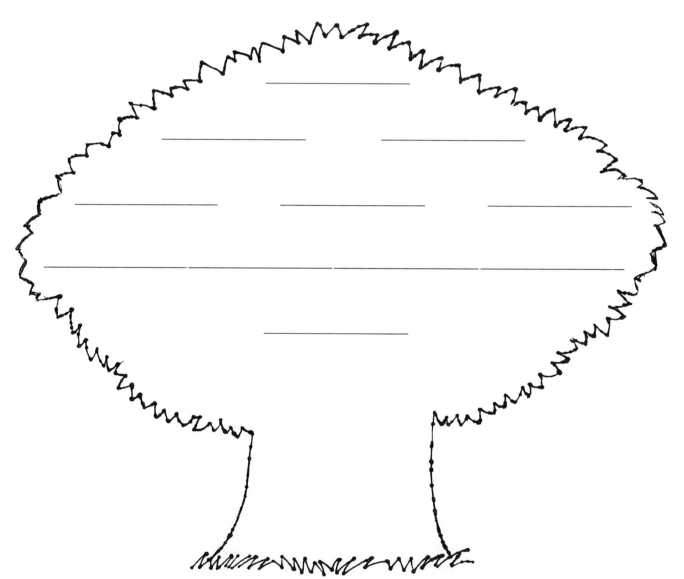

Read your poem to a friend.

Say "please."

A. Jamie would like a lot of things. Help her ask for what she
wants. Write questions using the word *please.*
See the example.

I would like some ice cream.

<u>Could I please have some ice cream?</u> _____

1. I would like to use your pencil.

_____

_____ ?

2. I would like a new watch.

_____

_____ ?

3. I would like a glass of water.

_____

_____ ?

B. Write two questions asking for something you would like.
Don't forget to use the word *please!*

1. _____ ?

2. _____ ?

Writing Objectives

1. Recognize appropriate sentence construction within the context of a written message.
2. Recognize appropriate English usage within the context of a written passage.
3. Recognize appropriate spelling, capitalization, and punctuation within the context of a written passage.

Clues

1. Read carefully to determine the best choice to replace incomplete sentences, run-ons, or subject-verb agreement.
2. Identify spelling, capitalization, or punctuation errors. You will not have to correct them.

Samples

| 1. People need trees for many reasons. |
| 2. People eat fruts that grow on trees. |

1. Read the first sentence in the box and mark the kind of mistake. If there is no mistake, mark **D.**

   (A) Spelling

   (B) Capitalization

   (C) Punctuation

   (D) No mistake

2. Read the second sentence and mark the kind of mistake. If there is no mistake, mark **D.**

   (A) Spelling

   (B) Capitalization

   (C) Punctuation

   (D) No mistake

If you chose **D No mistake** for number 1, you are correct. Number 2 has a spelling error. The word **fruts** should be **fruits.** The answer is **A.**

Name _____

Try It!

Directions

Mark the kind of mistake or correction for each sentence in the box. If there is no mistake, mark **D**.

---

1. Sometimes people cut down trees to sell the wood or clear the land when they do not plant new trees the forests disappear.

2. The rain forests in Brazil ———— disappearing.

3. Lumba companies cut down trees.

4. Ranchers cut down trees to raise cattle?

---

1. Which is the best choice for the first sentence?

   (A) Sometimes, people cut down the trees to sell the wood. Or clear the land when they do not plant new trees.

   (B) Sometimes people cut down trees. To sell the wood or clear the land when they do not plant new trees.

   (C) Sometimes, people cut down trees to sell the wood or clear the land. When they do not plant new trees, the forests disappear.

   (D) No mistake

2. Which word should be used to fill in the blank in sentence 2?

   (A) can

   (B) are

   (C) went

   (D) No mistake

3. What kind of mistake is in sentence 3?

   (A) Spelling

   (B) Capitalization

   (C) Punctuation

   (D) No mistake

4. What kind of mistake is in sentence 4?

   (A) Spelling

   (B) Capitalization

   (C) Punctuation

   (D) No mistake

Which way are you going?

Fill in the missing directions on the compass rose. Use the words on the suitcase.

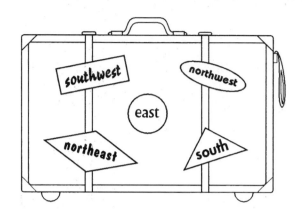

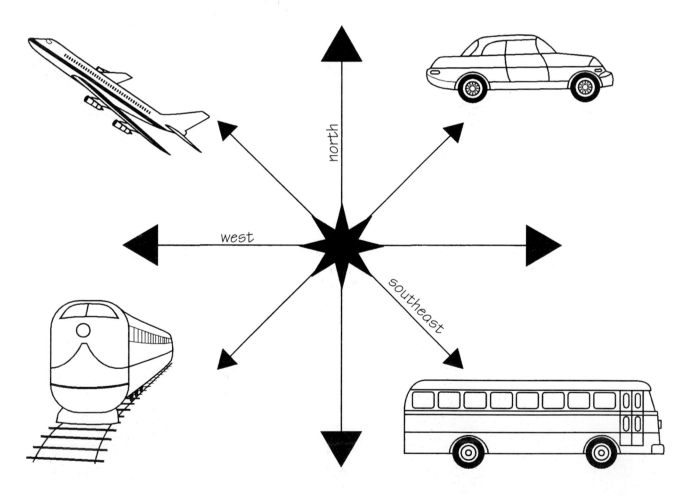

Name _____

More than One

A. Choose a word from the word box to complete the sentence.

| cities countries factories histories libraries |

1. People who work in _____ manufacture
   products.

2. New York and Boston are large _____ in
   the Northeast.

3. People go to _____ to take out books.

4. Mario has lived in two _____, Mexico
   and the United States.

5. Our class is learning about _____ of
   states.

B. Write two sentences.
   Use one word from the word box in each sentence.

_____ .

_____ .

Name _____

Florida is fun!

A. Read the questions and write the answers.

  1. What is the capital of Florida? _____

  2. Where can you find alligators? _____

  3. What does the word *Florida* mean? _____

  4. What region is Florida in? _____

  5. What three kinds of animals do you find in a marine park?

  _____

  6. What is an important crop in Florida? _____

B. Find the answers across and down in the puzzle and circle them.

```
A G Q F A T E P B F E
C S L S E A L S G D V
I H O B G L D E O H E
D H R U M L I L C K R
O O A R T A P C I J G
L N N S W H A L E S L
P T G U I A J K D W A
H V E N F S E J U V D
I W S Z N S O U T H E
N F L O W E R S P K S
S Z M A B E Q X R L S
```

Capital Letters

A. Rewrite the following sentences.
   Remember to begin each place name with a capital letter.

   1. The everglades is a park in florida.

   _____

   2. orlando is north of miami.

   _____

   3. The capital of florida is tallahassee.

   _____

B. Write your own sentences using proper nouns.

   1. What city and state do you live in?

   _____

   2. What region of the United States do you live in?

   _____

   3. What city and country does your family come from?

   _____

Name _____

Sh . . .

A. Say *nation* and *show.* Listen to the /sh/ sound.
   Read each group of words.
   Mark an X on the words that do not have the /sh/ sound.

1. fast	shoes	fish	short
2. apples	addition	ocean	older
3. station	start	musician	music
4. sunshine	dish	supper	doctor
5. ship	sunny	sing	social
6. name	national	share	special

B. Practice saying this tongue twister with a partner:
   She sells seashells by the seashore.

Name _____

How many?

A. Look at each picture. Fill in the blank with the correct word or words.

1. _____ of these pieces of fruit are apples.

    Some / Most

2. There are _____ trees in this forest.

    each / a lot of

3. Jack ate _____ of the bananas.

    each / most

4. _____ student has a notebook.

    Some / Each

B. Write a sentence using *some.* Then write a sentence using *most.*

_____

_____

Making Polite Requests

Work with a partner.
Match the polite request with the answer. Then read them to each other.

1. Can you tell me where the bathroom is, please?

   a. Sure. We'll eat lunch at noon.

2. Can you tell me what time we will eat lunch, please?

   b. Yes. Just push this button and it will start.

   c. Sure. It's at the end of the hall.

3. Excuse me, could you tell me how to use this machine?

Draw a polite request.

Choose a polite request. Draw a picture to go with it.

Name _____

Social Studies Objective: Demonstrate an understanding of geographical concepts and information.

Clues

1. Some questions will ask about regions of the United States and the resources that are found in them.

2. Other questions will ask for information associated with cities or states.

Sample

In which city does the President of the United States live?

(A) New York City

(B) Washington, D.C.

(C) Los Angeles

(D) Chicago

If you chose **Washington, D.C.,** you made the correct answer choice.

Name _____

Try It!

Directions
Read each question and all of the possible responses. Mark the best
response to each question.

1. In which region are cotton, peanuts, and oranges grown?

   Ⓐ the Northeast

   Ⓑ the Midwest

   Ⓒ the West

   Ⓓ the South

2. What does the West have that other regions do not have?

   Ⓐ copper and oil

   Ⓑ corn and wheat

   Ⓒ rice and cotton

   Ⓓ a lot of factories

3. Which of these places would you probably *not* find on a state map?

   Ⓐ a body of water

   Ⓑ a large park

   Ⓒ the capital city

   Ⓓ the street where you live

4. Which of these would probably *not* be a state symbol?

   Ⓐ a flower

   Ⓑ a tree

   Ⓒ a person

   Ⓓ a flag

Name _____

What is the order?

A. Draw a line to match the number with the word.

31   ninth

23   fourth

4   first

2   thirty-first

1   twenty-third

6   tenth

10   sixth

9   second

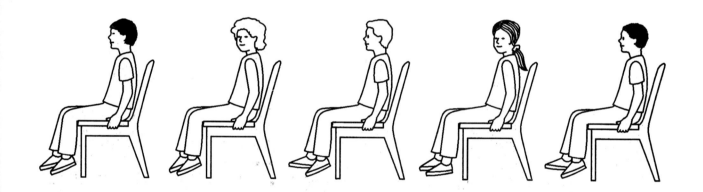

B. Draw a circle around the third student.
   Draw a square around the fifth student.

In the Past

Write the **past tense** verb form in the blank.

1. Some visitors _____ to our class yesterday.
   come / came

2. My father _____ us to school this morning.
   drive / drove

3. We _____ a house last year.
   built / build

4. She _____ the food to school.
   take / took

5. Last week, the people _____ happy.
   are / were

6. I didn't know the answer to the puzzle. I _____.
   give up / gave up

Prefixes

A. Add a prefix to make a new word. See the example.

re + new   = ___renew___

New Word

re + built   = _____

re + tell   = _____

re + name   = _____

re + write   = _____

re + fill   = _____

B. Use the new words to finish the sentences.

1. People _____ the city of San Francisco.

2. Please pick up your paper and _____ it.

3. Carlos will _____ the story to the children.

4. Rose's brother didn't like the name *Spot,* so she had to _____ her dog.

5. Could you _____ my glass of water, please?

Reading a Graph

The students in Mrs. Wong's fourth grade class made this graph.
Read the graph. Answer the questions.

Pets Students Have

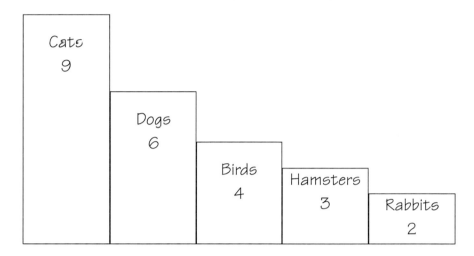

Cats
9

Dogs
6

Birds
4

Hamsters
3

Rabbits
2

What does this graph show?

_____

How many students have cats? _____

How many more students have cats than birds? _____

Are there more birds or rabbits as pets? _____

Words That Compare

1. Circle the picture that shows the **fewest** books.

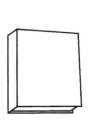 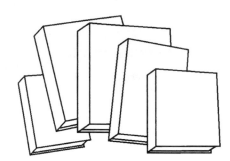 

2. Circle the picture that shows the **most** pencils.

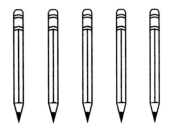 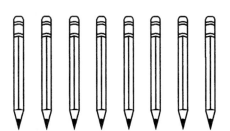 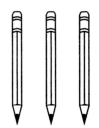

3. Circle the **biggest** desk.

4. Draw two circles in the box.

5. Draw more than two circles.

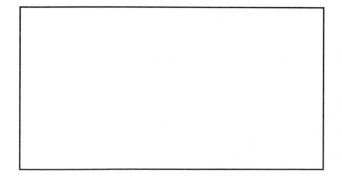 

Thinking About *th* Sounds

Listen as your teacher reads each word in the word box.

Decide what kind of *th* sound it has. Write the word in the correct column.

father	that	these	think
thanks	the	thin	thirty

th in *thing*	*th* in *this*

Name _____

I want to . . ., I'd like to . . .

A. Carmen wanted to be an artist. What do you want to be?

Draw a picture of what you want to be.

Then complete the sentence.

```

```

I want to be _____.

B. Carmen liked to go up on the roof on summer nights. What would you like to do?

Draw a picture of something you would like to do.

Then complete the sentence.

```

```

I'd like to _____.

Name _____

Where are the *qu* words?

Find and circle the following words across and down in the wordsearch.
Read the words aloud.

equal	queen	quilt
quarter	question	quiz

```
A V L M Q U I L T
R L E Q U A L M U
K D W U E N E F B
T J K I S B C N D
I N T Z T O C V O
Y E X H I A U G E
Q E S I O Z H Q P
Q U E E N G W S F
T Q U A R T E R R
```

Social Studies Objective: Demonstrate an understanding of historical concepts and information.

Clues

1. Some questions will ask you to show an understanding of the concept of change over time.
2. Other questions will ask you to recall basic facts about the history of California.

Sample

What were the people called who went to California in search of gold?

    Ⓐ the fifty-niners

    Ⓑ the gold diggers

    Ⓒ the forty-niners

    Ⓓ the gold seekers

If your answer is **the forty-niners,** you are correct.

Name _____

Try It!

Directions

Read each question carefully. Then mark the best answer choice.

1. What does a time line usually show?

   (A) events and their dates in the order in which they happened

   (B) locations of cities and states

   (C) names of important people and where they are from

   (D) increases in the population

2. The first people to live in California and in many other states were

   (A) people from Spain

   (B) American Indians

   (C) people from Russia

   (D) people from the Northeast

3. What was the main reason many explorers came to what is now the United States?

   (A) They wanted to hunt for food.

   (B) They wanted to travel.

   (C) They wanted to find riches.

   (D) They wanted to make new friends.

4. To which country did California belong before it became a state?

   (A) England

   (B) Spain

   (C) China

   (D) Mexico

Word Log

These are words that I want to learn to use.

_____   _____
_____   _____
_____   _____
_____   _____
_____   _____
_____   _____
_____   _____
_____   _____
_____   _____
_____   _____
_____   _____
_____   _____
_____   _____
_____   _____
_____   _____
_____   _____
_____   _____
_____   _____
_____   _____
_____   _____

Name _____

Word Log

These are words that I want to learn to use.

_____   _____

_____   _____

_____   _____

_____   _____

_____   _____

_____   _____

_____   _____

_____   _____

_____   _____

_____   _____

_____   _____

_____   _____

_____   _____

_____   _____

_____   _____

_____   _____

_____   _____

Word Log

These are words that I want to learn to use.

_____ _____

_____ _____

_____ _____

_____ _____

_____ _____

_____ _____

_____ _____

_____ _____

_____ _____

_____ _____

_____ _____

_____ _____

_____ _____

_____ _____

_____ _____

_____ _____

_____ _____